Straight On To Stardust

Also by Craig Lancaster

Novels

600 Hours of Edward
The Summer Son
Edward Adrift
The Fallow Season of Hugo Hunter
This Is What I Want
Edward Unspooled
Julep Street
You, Me & Mr. Blue Sky (with Elisa Lorello)
And It Will Be a Beautiful Life
Coming soon: Dreaming Northward

Short stories

The Art of Departure

STRAIGHT ON TO STARDUST

a play by
Craig Lancaster

MISSOURI BREAKS PRESS

Copyright © 2023 by Craig Lancaster

All rights reserved. No part of this book may be reproduced in any form or by any electronic or mechanical means, including information storage and retrieval systems, without permission in writing from the publisher, except by a reviewer, who may quote brief passages in a review. Scanning, uploading, and electronic distribution of this book or the facilitation of such without the permission of the publisher is prohibited. Your support of the author's rights is appreciated. Any member of educational institutions wishing to photocopy part or all of the work for classroom use, or anthology, should send inquiries to Missouri Breaks Press, 1219 Frost Street, Billings, MT 59105. Such inquiries will be looked upon favorably.

CAUTION: *Straight On to Stardust* is subject to a royalty. It is fully protected under the copyright laws of the United States and all countries covered by the International Copyright Union, the Pan-American Copyright Convention, and the Universal Copyright Convention. All rights, including professional, amateur, motion picture, recitation, public reading, radio broadcasting, television, video or sound taping, all other forms of mechanical or electronic reproduction, such as information storage and retrieval systems and photocopying, and rights of translation into foreign languages, are strictly reserved.

First-class professional, stock, and amateur applications for permission to perform it, and those other rights stated above, must be made in advance, before rehearsals begin, to the author: Craig Lancaster, 1219 Frost Street, Billings, MT 59105.

Printed in the United States of America

ISBN: 979-8-218-22106-5

*This play is dedicated to my father, Ron Lancaster.
He has done the hard work to ensure that it will
never be the two of us in that truck.*

Straight On To Stardust

Cast of Characters

Clinton Cobb (*mid-forties, blue-collar man*)
Jimmy Cobb, elder (*late seventies*)
Jimmy Cobb, younger (*mid-thirties or so*)
Kay Cobb (*twenties*)
Janine Cobb (*forties*)
Carolina Cobb (*early thirties*)
Gil Allen (*seventies/eighties*)
Brian Shamley (*ten to twelve*)
Man 1 (*mortuary worker*)
Man 2 (*mortuary worker*)
Convenience store clerk
Officer Jonathon Hunter
Susan Cobb (*invalid*)

Casting notes: For Sammy the Dog, Susan Cobb, and the party guests, it's easy enough to reduce headcount and just suggest their presence. The elder and younger versions of Jimmy Cobb never share the stage and thus can be occupied by one cast member. A small troupe could consolidate the roles of Man 1, Man 2, convenience store clerk, and Officer Hunter.

ACT ONE

Scene One

The opening is outdoors, winter, swirling snow and the screaming of wind. A man, north of forty years old, CLINTON COBB, *stands at the rear of his late-model pickup truck. He wears a canvas work coat, like you'd see on a construction crew member or pipeline worker—something blue-collar and marked by the rigors of the job.*

CLINTON *pulls the collar up and watches as two men come onto the stage, team-carrying a rigid, white-zippered bag.* CLINTON *lowers the tailgate and pops open the bed cover. He steps back and gives the men room.*

CLINTON: Just set him in there however he'll go.

[*The men grapple with the body bag, pushing and*

hefting, until it's fully in the bed of the pickup. When one of the men goes to close the bed cover, CLINTON *steps back in.]*

CLINTON: I've got 'er. She can be a little tricky.

[He closes the cover with a knowing flourish and locks it. He turns to the men. One hands him a clipboard, and CLINTON *signs his name, then looks at the man.]*

You get many like this?

MAN 1: A few. Not many. And not this time of year. It unnerves most folks, hauling somebody around.

CLINTON: He's not somebody anymore, I suppose.

MAN 1: No, I suppose not.

[The second man leaves. The first lingers. From the cab of the truck comes a low, guttural whine. Then a bark. Clinton raps the body of the truck with his hand.]

CLINTON: You just hold on.

[He turns again to the man with the clipboard.]

So that's it, then?

MAN 1: Pretty much.

[MAN 1 *pulls loose a duplicate of the paperwork from the perforation and hands it to* CLINTON.]

The body will be fine for the trip. The cold will help. There might still be some emissions, though.

CLINTON: Emissions?

MAN 1: Gases. Odors. Not much in this cold, I'd guess, but I wanted you to be aware should you have to open—

CLINTON: Nobody's opening nothing until he gets to where he's going.

MAN 1: Very well.

CLINTON: He's staying right where he is.

MAN 1: I understand.

[CLINTON *fixes the man with a stare.*]

CLINTON: OK, then.

[CLINTON *offers a handshake. It's not immediately accepted, a minor offense.*]

MAN 1: Albuquerque's a long way, is what I'm saying—

CLINTON: I'm aware.

MAN 1: I mean, you sure you don't want us to ship him? It'd be much simpler for you. Probably wouldn't cost much more, either.

[CLINTON *juts his hand insistently.* MAN 1 *gets the message and meets him, and* CLINTON's *hand swallows his.*]

CLINTON: Thanks just the same. Cost isn't my concern. Emissions, either.

[MAN 1 *exits from where he came.* CLINTON *leans his weight into the back of the pickup, setting his arms across the bed cover and his chin atop his gloved hands.*]

CLINTON: Simpler, my ass. [*He regards the truck, as if talking to the dead man inside.*] It wasn't ever gonna be that, was it?

[*He pushes himself up, disengaging from the truck bed and its grim cargo. He steps away and addresses the audience.*]

And after, hell, fourteen years of living here, it wasn't gonna be a plot at Mountview Cemetery, either. No way. Or, Jesus, cremation, which would have been a fitting end for the likes of this one. Assholes to ashes, dust to dust. No, he's gotta go back to Albuquerque, and I gotta take him. [*He turns and calls out to the truck.*] You were clear enough about that, weren't you?

[*He returns his gaze to the audience.*] That hunk of mortuary fodder back there is Jimmy Cobb, James Ardmore Cobb, nineteen-hundred and thirty-two to just here yesterday. Why they tagged him with a middle name that shares a town in Oklahoma, I'll never know. Anyway, he arrived in winter, left in winter, so I guess you could say his timing is exquisite. You could say that, if you didn't know him. And I suppose you didn't. You lucky sonsabitches.

[*The low whine comes again from the cab of the truck.* CLINTON *glances over, annoyed.*]

CLINTON: I know, boy.

[*He goes back to the tailgate and gives it a tug, making sure it's secure.*]

Well, old man, you'll get your wish. And I'll get mine, won't I?

[CLINTON *climbs into the cab of the pickup. The light goes down on them softly. From an adjacent stage, a twenty-something woman,* KAY COBB, *emerges. The spotlight settles on her, with* CLINTON, *as if driving, in the softer glow nearby.* KAY *gestures toward the truck.*]

KAY: That's my father, Clinton Cobb. The sentient,

breathing one in the cab, I mean, not the remains in the bed of it.

The story of any family, I suppose, is this odd stew of what we know to be true, what we've been told, and what we have to imagine—on evidence both solid and scant—to make sense of the gulfs between the two. So it is with this story of this family. My family. I know some things. Others know other things. In some cases, we've compared notes and tried to divine the likely truths between the lines. In other cases, we just don't know, and the details that might provide illumination have been carried off to places where they're unlikely to be found. Graves and other deep places, you might say.

Keep that in mind as you consider what's to come. Not everything is as it seems. But everything is. You follow?

[KAY *steps back, out of the spotlight, and the scene dims.*]

Scene Two

The opening is in a restaurant, a greasy-spoon kind of place with naugahyde booths and Western art on the walls. CLINTON *sits on one side of the booth, and a man thirty-five years older,* JIMMY COBB, *sits on the other. Their postures are rigid, defensive. There is no closeness here.*

JIMMY *sets his fork into a cutlet on his plate to hold it secure, then he draws his knife across the meat, sawing off a hunk. He takes a napkin and unfolds it on the table, then carefully wraps the piece of meat. He places the napkin in his shirt pocket, then leans back.* CLINTON *points at Jimmy's plate.*

CLINTON: You finished?

JIMMY: Yeah. I don't eat much anymore.

[CLINTON *lifts a glass of water and drinks deep. He uses the back of his hand to wipe his mouth.*]

CLINTON: What are you gonna do today?

JIMMY: Same old.

CLINTON: Yeah. Me, too.

[JIMMY *tilts his head back a bit, as if to frame* CLINTON *in his bifocals.*]

JIMMY: Thanks for lunch.

CLINTON: Always happy to buy for two. The vet know you're feeding your dog that way?

JIMMY: You know where my burial paperwork is, right?

CLINTON: Yeah. Why?

JIMMY: It's in the little safe on the TV stand.

CLINTON: Yeah, Dad, I know.

JIMMY: The key is—

CLINTON: Behind the silverware tray. I know.

[CLINTON *scratches at his watch face, avoiding the penetrating stare from* JIMMY, *then finally looks up.*]

What brought this on?

JIMMY: That's right. Behind the silverware.

CLINTON: Yeah. You told me.

JIMMY: Just sit still. I ain't gonna keep you much longer from places you'd rather be.

CLINTON: Dad…

JIMMY: OK. You don't have to do anything but get me down there. Put me in my truck and drive me. They'll take care of the rest.

CLINTON: We've been over this.

JIMMY: Everything's arranged.

CLINTON: I know.

JIMMY: I bought the plot and the headstone before you made me move here.

CLINTON: I know.

JIMMY: I've got the music and the sermon all picked out.

CLINTON: I know.

JIMMY: Flowers. You don't have to do anything.

CLINTON: I know, Dad.

JIMMY: Am I boring you?

CLINTON: No. But why are you bringing it up now? We've been over it. Many times.

JIMMY: I just want to make sure, for when the time comes. I'm no spring chicken.

CLINTON: No, you're straight-up gristle.

[CLINTON *looks over the rim of his coffee cup and smiles.* JIMMY *stares grimly back, until* CLINTON *averts his eyes.*]

JIMMY: Bring Sammy. He'd like a nice ride through the countryside.

[CLINTON *reaches across the table and pats* JIMMY's *shirt pocket, holding the meat.* JIMMY *withdraws, agitated at the intrusion.*]

CLINTON: The way you feed him, that dog will die of diabetes long before you're gone.

JIMMY: Never you mind that. He likes it.

[JIMMY, *clearly offended, drinks his water, and* CLINTON *stands up from the booth and walks away, facing and addressing the audience.*]

CLINTON: I wouldn't have been so hard on him if I'd known what was coming and how soon it would arrive. And, yeah, so I'm a big baby to keep banging away at that damn dog of his. I mean, it's a dog, and here I am, purportedly a grown-ass man. We ain't of the same species. We ain't in a struggle for superiority; that question has been decided for all time. It's unseemly, I know, but that dog saw more of the man's good nature than I ever did. Let me tell you, if dogs went to college, Sammy's fund would have been filled to the brimming. That's what I'm saying. Do I hold a grudge? Against the dog and the man? Damn right. Am I silly for holding it? Also damn right, at least as far as the dog is concerned. The man had it coming.

Anyway, what's done is done. And what's not isn't and never will be. Let's move on.

[*The scene dims.*]

Scene Three

The scene opens with CLINTON *in his truck, driving.* KAY *appears on an adjacent stage, for the audience to see as she speaks into her cellular phone.*

KAY: I'd have gone with you. All you had to do was ask. Or tell me.

CLINTON: No reason. You're busy. It'll just take a few days.

KAY: Dad—

CLINTON: Look, Katey, it's no big deal.

KAY: Kay.

CLINTON: I know. Sorry.

[*Silence lingers.* CLINTON *reaches into the passenger area and scratches the dog, Sammy, behind the ears.*]

KAY: I guess I just don't get it.

CLINTON: That makes two of us.

KAY: You're consistently glib, Dad. I'll give you that.

CLINTON: I'm not—

KAY: Look, I just don't think this is a good time for you to be alone. I would have come. I would have wanted to come. I wished you'd asked me.

CLINTON: I know.

KAY: I'd have been there if I'd known you were going to do something like this. But, I guess you'd have had to say something, and, well—

CLINTON: I should have. I'm sorry.

KAY: You're halfway to Sheridan. Easy to say you're sorry now.

[CLINTON *bites down on an urge to respond, to keep it going. He scratches the dog again.*]

KAY: Grandpa's really in the back of the pickup?

CLINTON: Yeah, he's back there. Bagged for freshness.

KAY: Don't say that.

CLINTON: I owe you another "sorry." I should buy them in bulk at Costco.

KAY: Isn't that weird? Having him back there like that?

CLINTON: I don't know what's weird or not.

KAY: Well, that's not especially deep, is it?

CLINTON: I can't be sorry and deep at the same time.

[*Silence settles in again.*]

KAY: I wish I'd known him better.

CLINTON: A lot of people wish that, except the people who're sorry they knew him too well. Maybe you ought to consider the grace of your situation and count your blessings. Deep enough for you?

KAY: Again with the lines. It's like you can't help yourself. But I know you can. That's what's so frustrating.

CLINTON: I don't mean to frustrate you.

KAY: Whatever. Yeah, you do. Listen, though. Call mom. I think you hurt her feelings.

CLINTON: Of course I did. It's what I do.

[KAY *has had enough. She hangs up the phone without a goodbye.* CLINTON, *chastened, grimly turns his attention back to the road. He cranes his neck to peer out the driver's-side window.*]

CLINTON: Getting bad. Hope this snow doesn't hang us up.

[CLINTON *reaches again for the dog, who mumbles contentedly.*]

You're missing the countryside, you know. Such as it is. It's the whole reason he wanted you to come. If you were gonna sleep the whole way, you could have stayed home and ordered pizza.

[*Another several-second pause*]

That's a joke, Sammy.

Maybe it's not the same thing for you—you're just a dog, and besides, the old bastard cut your nuts off before you had the chance—but lemme tell you about being a dad. The first thing you think of is how much better you want to do it than what was done to you. You hear me? You find out you're getting one of these humans, you spend nine months imagining who or what they'll be, you project out a lifetime—your best hope of one, mind you—before they've even drawn breath in the world, and you tag them with a name to keep them sorted out from everyone else. We had one lined up before she even showed up. Katey. A good, solid name. We put some damn thought into that one. We could see her in our mind's eye, and wouldn't you know it, she looked like a Katey. Came out, cried like a Katey. Pooped like a Katey. It fit, that name.

[CLINTON *looks to the dog and shakes his head.*]

But it turns out later that the kid has her own ideas about who she is and what she'll go by, thank you very much, and what can you do? Nothing. It's her name, not yours. Kay Cobb. It sounds like a salad or something, doesn't it? All right, kid. Whatever you say.

[CLINTON *leans forward, peering through the windshield.*]

Gas station coming. You need to go pee?

[*The dog woofs.*]

I do, too. [*Long pause*] I wish you could talk, Sammy. [*A shorter pause*] But I imagine you couldn't have gotten a word in edgewise with that old rascal, so why bother, right?

Well, boy, if you have anything to say, you let me know, all right? Meantime, I'll just keep pushing us along. I must have been a fool to take this on. You know what I mean?

[CLINTON *looks to the dog as if expecting an answer.*]

You're a good listener, Sammy. Be proud of that.

[*The scene dims.*]

Scene Four

The scene opens in a convenience store, with CLINTON *pushing items across to a* CASHIER—*two hot dogs and a large drip coffee. The* CASHIER *is laconic, almost dismissive, and* CLINTON *is impatient.*

CASHIER: That your dog that took a crap out there?

CLINTON: I wouldn't call him mine. We're just traveling together. We alternate the driving.

CASHIER: I—

CLINTON: We alternate the music, too. I play Merle Haggard. Dog likes Mozart. He doesn't look like much, but he's cultured.

CASHIER: Look, man, you gonna clean it up? I'm so sick of it, you people who just let your dogs crap all over the place—

CLINTON: The shit you have to put up with, right?

CASHIER: Seriously. [*A pause, as he catches up to* CLINTON's *mocking.*] Hey, man, you trying to be funny?

CLINTON: No. Was I?

CASHIER: Was you what?

CLINTON: Funny?

CASHIER: Just clean it up, OK, man?

CLINTON: I'll clean it up, sure enough, but a man has to work himself up to such an endeavor, and I feel a little peaked. You got a place where I can eat this delicious meal? I do believe that without sustenance, well, I'd just faint dead away at the sheer exhilaration of sweeping up the rectal discharge of that fine animal out there.

[*The* CASHIER, *annoyed and defeated, points to a small table and chair in the corner, then leaves his post.* CLINTON, *self-satisfied, settles in. He eats the hot dogs, three quick bites each, and then takes a long draw from the coffee. It's been a long drive, only to get longer. He looks at the audience, weary, and shows his cellphone, then begins speaking.*]

CLINTON: I hate these damn things. You love

them, I know, damn near couldn't live without them, because, hey, if you need to find out what year *Smoke On The Water* came out or how far it is from Glendive to Milwaukee, it's right there at your fingertips. And that's great, as far as it goes, but this [*he waves the phone for the audience*] about tripled the chances I'd be talking with people I don't want to talk to, at times when I don't want to talk to them. Did you ever consider what you were giving up when you agreed to be forever reachable? I don't think you did.

[CLINTON *punches a number into the phone, holds it to his ear, and waits. On an adjacent stage,* JANINE COBB *steps under a spotlight, holding her own phone.*]

JANINE: Where are you?

CLINTON: Sheridan. Katey said you wanted me to call.

JANINE: You doing OK?

CLINTON: Sure.

JANINE: Snowing?

CLINTON: Janine, there's a whole channel devoted to the weather, so if you really care, I suggest you tune in. What do you want?

JANINE: When were you going to tell me about Jimmy?

CLINTON: I figured Katey would. She did, right?

JANINE: She did, clearly, since you did not, otherwise how would I know? But come on, Clinton. He was my father-in-law for twenty-one years. You could have called and let me know.

CLINTON: And you shared a city with him for four years after that and couldn't be bothered. What do you want from me?

JANINE: The same thing I've always wanted from you, Clinton, and that's just one consideration for what I might want or need before you go off and do what you're going to do anyway. Who knows? Maybe it'll actually change your trajectory one of these days. I won't hold my breath.

CLINTON: Jesus.

JANINE: Fine. Fine. I want nothing. [*She says this staccato and emotionless.* CLINTON *takes one deep breath, then another.*]

CLINTON: I'm sorry I didn't call. OK? I'm sorry I didn't ask Katey to come. OK?

JANINE: I just wish you wouldn't make it so hard for her.

CLINTON: Jesus, Janine, I'm trying to make it easier.

I just want to get Dad down there and be done with it. I'm trying to do what he wants—what I stupidly promised him I'd do—without tangling anybody else up in it. That's all.

[*The ferocity of the exchange lays bare the weight of history on both of them.* CLINTON *seems breathless.* JANINE *lets the burn sink in and dissipate before she continues.*]

JANINE: Did he suffer much? I'd hate it if he suffered.

CLINTON: I don't know. Massive stroke, they said. I don't know if that hurt much. Wasn't a lot to do after I found him. He was in the ICU for a day, and he just kind of went to sleep.

JANINE: I'm glad for that, at least.

CLINTON: It's like he knew. Talked about his funeral the day before. Wouldn't shut up about it, honestly.

JANINE: He always talked about his funeral. I think it's the one thing he looked forward to. [*She laughs, realizing the absurdity.*] That's weird, since—

CLINTON: I know.

JANINE: This will sound bad, I know, but at least it's over, right? His burden is gone. Yours, too. He was so angry at the world, seemed like.

CLINTON: Me. He was angry at me.

JANINE: He resented you because he couldn't care for himself, that's all.

CLINTON: OK, whatever.

JANINE: What?

CLINTON: Nothing.

JANINE: What, Clint?

CLINTON: Just leave it. I gotta go.

JANINE: So go, then. You're not going the whole way today, I hope.

CLINTON: No. Colorado Springs maybe. Hopefully. The rest tomorrow.

JANINE: OK. Be careful.

CLINTON: Always am. Bye.

[CLINTON *ends the call and stands.* JANINE *recedes.* CLINTON *shakes the stilled cellphone at the audience.*]

CLINTON: I hate these damn things. Can't say that would have gone any better if we'd been face-to-face, though, and it might well have gone worse. The phone [*he looks at the item in his hand*] gives some distance, at least, some detachment. Janine and me, we needed that, when it came right down to it. Too much pain when we were in proximity. Too much we both knew and remembered and couldn't shake loose from. Too much love, too, if that makes any sense. Sometimes, I'll be thinking about things and say to myself, "You know, I wish Janine was here so I could tell her about this," and then I realize she's not, and so I look at the phone and think, "Well, I could call her," but I know that wouldn't be the same, so I don't.

[*He looks at the phone in his hand again.*]

You're good for something, I guess.

[CLINTON *places his trash in the can, then heads over to the stage where the truck sits. He scans around, alights on something, then uses a hand covered by a plastic bag to sweep up a handful from the ground. He turns toward the store, showing it. The* CASHIER, *back at his post, offers mocking applause.* CLINTON *throws the bag away and gets into the cab. The scene dims.*]

Scene Five

As the scene opens, KAY *steps forward from her position on an adjacent stage, and a single spotlight finds her.*

KAY: So let me tell you about the prototypical interaction between my mother and my father, whether they stood in the same room or talked by way of cellular towers. Voices were never too pitched, emotions would simmer but rarely boil. Ultimately, there would be kindness in their words even when they'd come no closer to bridging the distances between them. It was annoying, really, because it was all so anticlimactic. You'd get the sense that, maybe, we were closing in on a watershed kind of anger, something cleansing, maybe even something terrible that might lead to some bit of higher ground, then the moment would lamentably pass. Cordiality, that most unsatisfying of manners, would set in again.

What was Dad thinking the day he drove off? I don't

know. I don't know because he didn't say. Dad wasn't a sphinx, exactly, but he also never managed to get rich collecting pennies for what was on his head. They say if you don't know what an extrovert thinks, you haven't listened, and if you don't know what an introvert thinks, you haven't asked. I listened. I asked. I don't even know if Dad was an introvert or an extrovert. That's how far in the weeds I was. We all were.

The most unkind thing I ever said to my father is that he didn't know the difference between being around and being present. It's also the most accurate thing I ever said to him. So I let it stand. And I'll keep it standing, even knowing what I don't know now. Because here's the hell of it: The not knowing is more profound.

[KAY *recedes, and the spotlight dims, then shifts to the stage where* CLINTON *sits in his truck, driving. Dusk has fallen outside. After a time, the spotlight widens, revealing a woman with clamorous hair, wearing fashions of the 1970s. This is* CAROLINA COBB, CLINTON's *mother. She has been dead for years.* CLINTON *looks over and regards her as if her sudden appearance is unsurprising to him.* CAROLINA *pets Sammy the dog.*]

CAROLINA: He always did like these hairy herding dogs.

CLINTON: That there is Sammy. It's been a long

while since he's herded anything other than kibble. Can't even take a run at the delivery guy now. Poor, impotent bastard.

CAROLINA: Lovely dog. He smells like week-old trash. [*She again pets Sammy.*] So you're taking him home, then?

CLINTON: Sammy?

CAROLINA: Your father. Don't play that game with me.

CLINTON: Yeah. I guess it's home. To him. Not to me. Where he wanted to go, so, you know, I'm the granter of wishes.

CAROLINA: You certainly were for me.

[CLINTON *flushes with warmth at his mother's kind words.*]

CAROLINA: I'm surprised he lasted this long. Seventy-nine?

CLINTON: Seventy-seven. You know this. You'd have been seventy-one. Don't play that game with me.

CAROLINA: Oh, Clinton. You always were such a clever child. It's annoying sometimes.

[*Some moments pass. They exude contentment at being together.*]

CAROLINA: You won't make it past Buffalo today, not in this weather.

CLINTON: I'll make it.

CAROLINA: Whatever you say.

[CLINTON *gives his mother a sideways glance, then reorients himself to the road.*]

CLINTON: I thought you might show. Glad you did.

CAROLINA: I thought you might have some questions. Thought I could be of some help.

CLINTON: No questions. Just thoughts, I guess.

CAROLINA: We accept that currency, too.

CLINTON: I don't know how to say it exactly. The thoughts are tangled up, every time I try to put some words to them.

CAROLINA: Just say it. We're beyond preambles, don't you think?

[CLINTON *tightens his grasp on the steering wheels, his hands at ten and two.*]

CLINTON: OK, look. It's not like I'm unhappy he lived as long as he did, but I can't help wondering how it's fair that I got so much time with him and so little with you. You know what I'm saying?

CAROLINA: I know.

CLINTON: You and I could have done more with that time than he and I ever did.

[CLINTON *looks again at his mother. She smiles warmly, then bends down for a closer look at Sammy.*]

CLINTON: Mom?

CAROLINA: I heard you, sweetie. It's hard to explain. Where I am, the concept of what's fair or not isn't as simple as it must seem to you. And time…well, time is both irrelevant and finely understood in a way it wasn't before.

CLINTON: I don't follow.

CAROLINA: Look. Circumstances aren't fair or unfair, OK? They just are. Things happen and don't happen, people are and they aren't, this and that comes and goes, and I think you want to find some sense to it that's simply not there sometimes. Do you understand?

CLINTON: Sort of. I guess.

CAROLINA: Let me put it this way. I don't think it was particularly fair that I got sick twenty years before the BRCA1 gene was discovered. But it wasn't unfair, either. It's just what happened. That's where my earthly life fell. I was angry, hurt, violated at the time. It makes better sense when you can see it in a sort of cosmic context.

CLINTON: So it's all chance? [*His anger flashes.*] That's no answer. I was eleven years old. I still needed you.

CAROLINA: I know. But it's like I've told you before: I've been here.

CLINTON: Not in the way I needed you to be. [*He closes his eyes, then opens them again, quick. He looks to her.*] I'm sorry. I don't mean to be hurtful.

CAROLINA: Nothing hurts. Say what you need to say.

CLINTON: That's it, I guess.

[*They ride on. Silence sets in. At last,* CAROLINA *speaks again.*]

CAROLINA: So he's in the back?

CLINTON: Yeah, he's in the back. Trapped, for once. The old bastard.

CAROLINA: There's something poetic in that.

CLINTON: How so?

CAROLINA: Oh, nothing. Sorry. Just some earthbound grudges stirring up. Forgive me.

CLINTON: So tell me this, at least. Did you love him?

CAROLINA: Sammy? [CLINTON, *highly amused, shakes his head.*] Did you?

CLINTON: I asked first.

CAROLINA: Yes, but I think your answer is more important than mine. You're still here.

CLINTON: Still, I want to know. I've always wondered. The longer I've lived and the longer you've been gone—I mean, somewhere else—the less sense it has made to me. I don't see how the two of you ever added up to anything.

CAROLINA: We've had lots of opportunities to talk about this. Why is it coming up now?

CLINTON: I don't know.

CAROLINA: Son...

CLINTON: I guess I always hoped he and I would

talk about it, but we never did. Now we never will.

[CAROLINA *considers this, then starts in again.*]

CAROLINA: Did you ever wonder why I showed up only sometimes? You never brought it up, so I never volunteered, but you were a perceptive boy, Clinton.

CLINTON: I was just glad to see you whenever.

CAROLINA: Well, there are rules. Rules of engagement, I guess you would call them. I wasn't permitted to come to you until you were grown up. That about killed me. No pun intended.

CLINTON: I see. What else?

CAROLINA: What I could say and not say. What I could reveal. Whether I could intervene, and I couldn't. So you and I, we just chatted. Like we did when you'd come home from school. You remember?

CLINTON: Sure.

CAROLINA: So let's chat. Did you love your father?

[CLINTON *regards her. He swallows hard, collecting his thoughts.*]

CLINTON: I think I did. I was his son, and he was my dad.

CAROLINA: That sounds like some sort of genetic obligation, not love. Little boys love their fathers. It's the way of things. Older boys...well, things sometimes change.

CLINTON: I guess.

CAROLINA: Give it some deeper thought. You have the time.

CLINTON: I will. Now you answer my question.

CAROLINA: Did I love Jimmy?

CLINTON: That's the one.

CAROLINA: I think so. I saw something in him that moved me, I think. Or maybe I just saw some good times in the backseat of a Chevy and—

CLINTON: Mom!

CAROLINA: Oh, please. You telling me you've never been in the backseat of a Chevy with a girl? Remember: I know more and have seen more than I'm telling you.

CLINTON: A Mazda. Once.

CAROLINA: Really?

CLINTON: With Janine. Up on the Rims. My legs dangling out of the back window. Small car, a Mazda.

CAROLINA: Sharp moves, son. Sharp moves. [*She points out the windshield.*] Snow gate's coming down. You're not making it past Buffalo tonight.

[*A frown screws up on CLINTON's face as he swings the truck hard for an exit. The spotlight narrows on him, casting CAROLINA into darkness.*]

CLINTON: Wait.

[*He reaches for the dog in the opposite seat.*]

Hold on to your ass, Sammy. Looks like we're gonna have to hunker down for the night.

[*The scene dims.*]

ACT TWO

Scene Six

As the scene opens, it's pitch-black on all three stages. On one, CLINTON sleeps in a hotel bed. A voice, from a being unseen, intones.

JIMMY'S VOICE: You might ought to get up now.

[*The lights come up, revealing* CLINTON, *who sits up and rubs his eyes, coming out of slumber. The truck, on the stage opposite him, can be seen in a single spotlight. Sammy, unseen, lets out a low, throaty grumble, and* CLINTON *scolds him softly.*]

CLINTON: Sammy.

[CLINTON *approaches where a window hangs and looks out at the truck. The dog continues grumbling.*]

Sammy, be quiet.

[CLINTON *looks more intently.*]

What the hell?

[CLINTON *goes to the bed and sits down, pulling on his boots. Sammy continues a low, guttural growl. CLINTON then crosses to the other stage and the pickup, in a hurry.*]

Hey!

[CLINTON *stares off at an unseen thief who's running away. He bends over and picks up the crowbar the thief has left behind. He waggles it in the direction the thief ran.*]

Lucky bastard. I'd have clouted you.

[CLINTON *goes to the tailgate and jostles it. It's clear the lock was broken, but the thief didn't get into the pickup bed before he was interrupted.*]

That was a damn dumb thing. I'm gonna have to fix that.

[*From the other stage, Sammy begins barking. Lights come up, as if from adjacent rooms.* CLINTON *hisses under his breath.*]

Sammy, shut up!

[CLINTON *returns to the motel room stage.* CLINTON *dresses, then crosses back to the truck. He opens the cab door and rummages in the backseat for heavy twine. He cuts off long pieces and uses that to secure the bed cover. Finished with the job, he returns to the motel room stage. When the lights come up there, a younger version of* JIMMY COBB *sits in a chair by the bed, waiting for him. He wears pressed western slacks, a button-front shirt with pearl snap buttons, and pointy-toed cowboy boots.*]

CLINTON: First Mom, now you. Who's the lucky boy?

[JIMMY *pitches forward, grabbing the armrests and looking around the room intently.* CLINTON *goes to his duffel bag and begins packing.*]

JIMMY: Carolina's here? I haven't been able to find her.

CLINTON: No, earlier.

JIMMY: Oh. I'll catch up to her eventually, I guess.

[CLINTON *walks past him and drops the duffel by the door.*]

CLINTON: I wouldn't know anything about that.

JIMMY: No, I guess you wouldn't. It's not what I expected, I'll tell you. Not that I expected anything, except maybe that I'd be barbecuing my nuts off right about now.

[JIMMY *plays with Sammy, who's sitting near him.*]

CLINTON: You look good. Surprising. You sure looked like shit last I saw you.

[JIMMY *holds out his arms and regards himself.*]

JIMMY: You like this? That was one of the perks, that I can pick my era any time I want. I always liked wearing these duds.

CLINTON: I'm thrilled for you.

JIMMY: You let that thief go.

CLINTON: I didn't let him go. He got away.

JIMMY: Whatever. Point is, you—

CLINTON: I don't want to hear it, OK? Your damn dog woke up everybody up, and now I gotta—

JIMMY: Don't you blame this good boy.

CLINTON: You're right. I blame you.

[CLINTON *crisscrosses the room, gathering sundries and other items he'll need to take out for a hasty exit.* JIMMY *sits, offended.*]

JIMMY: You should have let that guy finish getting back there with me. He'd have unzipped me—[*his hands do the scene in pantomime*]—and I'd have gone, "Boo, motherfucker!" Boy, howdy. That would have been something.

CLINTON: Yeah, that's all I need. You dead. Him, scared to death. Me, explaining to the cops why there are two dead bodies in the back of my truck.

[CLINTON *hefts his things and leaves the room, crossing over to the truck.* JIMMY *follows on his heels.* CLINTON *summons Sammy into the cab, then goes back to the tailgate.* JIMMY *follows again.*]

JIMMY: Go ahead and open me up. Let's take a look.

CLINTON: I was thinking about it.

JIMMY: Scared, though, ain't you?

CLINTON: I'm tired. I'm worn out with your bullshit. I'm gonna have to beat it out of here with a couple of hours of sleep, because I can't chance that somebody called the cops and I'm gonna have to explain the likes of you—the dead you, the better version—if they show up. So how about you just leave me alone?

JIMMY: No, no, let's take a drive.

[*JIMMY climbs into the cab with Sammy. CLINTON lingers at the back of the truck, caught by indecision. Finally, he climbs into the cab and starts the ignition. They drive silently for a time, then JIMMY points out the windshield.*]

JIMMY: Snow gate's still down. You won't make it.

CLINTON: I'll make it.

JIMMY: You'll get hung up in the median and they'll have to come pull your sorry ass out. Probably laugh at you.

CLINTON: I'll make it.

[*The engine revs and CLINTON lets out a whoop. He drives as if the truck is fighting him, fishtailing, as he whips around the highway gate and back onto the road. Sounds of snow churning and tires spitting.*]

CLINTON: Told you.

JIMMY: Luck.

CLINTON: Skill.

JIMMY: Whatever you say, Sport. Where's your mom? Can you get her here?

CLINTON: You think you'd be here if I had any control over that?

[CLINTON *looks at* JIMMY, *who's blank-faced in response.*]

JIMMY: That's a hell of a thing to say to your own father.

CLINTON: The truth hurts and all that.

JIMMY: You know what your problem is?

CLINTON: Present company excluded?

JIMMY: Don't be a smartass.

CLINTON: Tell me.

JIMMY: Your problem is you just don't know what you know. About anything. Ever.

CLINTON: What is this, tales from the cryptic?

JIMMY: You know exactly why I'm here.

CLINTON: Too ornery to die. I tried to tell the doctors.

JIMMY: See? I'm trying to tell you something, and all you've got is a smart mouth.

CLINTON: This is rich. You die, and I'm the one who ends up in hell.

JIMMY: Never mind. I'll be back. We'll see how much of a big talker you are then.

CLINTON: Don't go now. It's just getting fun.

[*The spotlight sharpens on* CLINTON. JIMMY *fades into darkness. A growl thrums in Sammy's throat.* CLINTON *reaches for the dog's head.*]

CLINTON: Come on now.

[*A louder growl, then a full-out bark and a snap, and* CLINTON *pulls back his hand, taking a stricken finger into his mouth, tasting the blood. In the next instant, he whips his hand back at the dog, whapping Sammy in the snout. The dog cries and whimpers. The dam breaks within* CLINTON, *and he weeps. The scene dims.*]

[*Intermission*]

Scene Seven

The scene opens with a single spotlight on KAY *as she steps forward and begins speaking directly with the audience.*

KAY: Mom waited until I was grown, gone, out of the house, in college, in my life, in my career before she told me that Dad talks to dead people.

[*She stops. Considers.*]

No, wait, let me say it as she did:

[JANINE *steps out, into a second spotlight, and she and* KAY *say the next line in unison.*]

Your father, he has visitations.

[JANINE *recedes, and it's just* KAY *under a single spotlight.*]

Of course, being *his* child if not *a* child, I wanted to know more. Is Dad delusional?

[JANINE *returns, under a spotlight. The two women face each other and have a conversation.*]

JANINE: Delusional? No.

KAY: Is Dad mentally ill?

JANINE: No.

KAY: Will Dad see somebody about this?

JANINE: What do you think, dear?

KAY: Do you believe Dad?

JANINE: Yes.

KAY: Should I believe Dad?

JANINE: Yes.

KAY: Can I talk to Dad about this?

JANINE: Absolutely not.

[*The spotlight goes off* KAY, *who continues standing in darkness.* JANINE *addresses the audience directly.*]

JANINE: There was no way to keep it from her, and I didn't want to, anyway. I was glad Clinton shared it with me—he pretty much had to, after I caught him talking to a wall—but I thought it unfair that he expected me to just hold it. Because every question Kay asked me, I had asked myself long before. It seems crazy, right? It seems fanciful and weird and invented, and I'd have said as much to Clinton if I'd thought he was lying to me.

But Clinton, whatever his faults, is not a liar. Sometimes, I wish he would have been. What came to pass between us, it might have been easier to take if I could consider him a dirty, deceitful liar. But I can't.

So Clinton told me, and I told our daughter, but that's where the telling ends, this little aside...well, aside.

But Kay, talking to her dad about it? I can't have that. Neither can he. Oh, he'd be ticked off something royal.

[*The spotlight on* JANINE *fades.* KAY *is illuminated again.*]

KAY: So I never said a word. And, truly, I mostly didn't think about it, because where does that lead? Nowhere good. I went about my life, as we all should. When Mom and Dad divorced—the biggest surprise in never, even if neither of them is capable of loving anyone else—I simply adjusted my course. I spent a little bit of Thanksgiving and Christmas with both of them, and a whole lot of everything else with my co-workers, my friends, the people I choose. I inherited these people. Do I love them? Yes, I do, with my whole heart. Would I choose them?

No. No, I would not.

But let me tell you something else.

[KAY *reaches into her pocket and withdraws a yellowed newspaper clipping. She begins reading it aloud.*]

Dateline: Casper, Wyoming. Three family members were found dead in their home Friday, victims of an apparent murder-suicide.

Dead are Martin Shamley, age thirty-three; his wife, Margaret, thirty-two; and twelve-year-old Brian Shamley, the couple's son.

Police say it appears that Martin Shamley shot his wife and son in the back of the head as they watched television, then turned the gun on himself.

No further details were offered.

I found this in a closet before I left for school in Missoula a few years ago. It was jammed into a 1979 *Reader's Digest* World Almanac like a bookmark. The date on the article: May 13th, 1978. In June of that year, Dad and Grandpa Jimmy moved from Casper, Wyoming, to New Mexico, my Grandma Carolina having died a few years earlier. Oh, how I wish I'd known her.

I asked Dad about this article when I found it. I said, "What's this about?" He was taciturn, as is his way.

[CLINTON *appears on another stage, under a second spotlight.*]

CLINTON: I knew Brian. Nice kid. Sad story.

[*The spotlight leaves* CLINTON, *casting him in darkness.*]

KAY: Like I said, he never got rich collecting pennies for his thoughts. Mom didn't have any answers, either, except maybe Occam's Razor—you know, the simplest explanation is probably the correct one.

[JANINE *steps out into a spotlight.*]

JANINE: It's an old clipping in an old book, honey. Probably somebody kept it and it floated around and...

[JANINE *shrugs and recedes into darkness.*]

KAY: A likely story.

[*The scene dims,* KAY *recedes, then the lights come up*

again, and CLINTON *is in his pickup, driving, holding his phone to his ear.* JANINE *steps out under a spotlight on an adjacent stage, with a cellphone to hers.]*

JANINE: They're calling it a mega-storm, Clint. We've already got fifteen inches on the ground, and it's still coming. You shouldn't be out there.

CLINTON: It's not so bad. No man's land now, so I just gotta keep plugging. Just gotta push through. Almost to Casper now.

JANINE: You should have flown. You'd be there. It'd be done.

CLINTON: I know. Next time, I'll do it that way.

JANINE: Next time? [*She catches herself, realizes he's being sly, then laughs.*] Oh, Clint. This is why, you know.

CLINTON: Why you loved me?

JANINE: Why I couldn't quite bring myself to shoot you.

CLINTON: Same difference.

[*They both laugh, full of mirth. It's a good exchange, one imbued with a spirit of happier times between them. But* CLINTON's *face takes on a darkening.*]

CLINTON: I need to talk to you about something.

JANINE: OK. Talk.

CLINTON: You know how you'd find me, you know, late at night and I was talking?

JANINE: Sleepwalking.

CLINTON: Something like that.

JANINE: Sure.

CLINTON: You remember that?

JANINE: I do. You're seeing her again, are you?

CLINTON: And him.

JANINE: *Him*, him?

CLINTON: My dad. Jimmy. Yes.

[*A pause of some length, as* JANINE *absorbs this.*]

JANINE: When?

CLINTON: In the truck. At the motel. A couple of hours ago.

JANINE: But they're not real.

CLINTON: They come and go. Real? I don't know.

JANINE: What do they say?

CLINTON: Oh, you know. She's gentle, kind, funny. He's an asshole. Same old.

JANINE: Well, that sounds real enough. [*She laughs, but it's for her own benefit, as she tries to gather her thoughts.*] Jesus, Clint, you're sleep-deprived, and you've got seven hundred miles to go. Why are you doing this? Just sleep it off and come home. He won't care. Not now.

CLINTON: I can't.

JANINE: Why not?

CLINTON: I told him I'd do this. I gave him my word.

JANINE: So you're keeping promises now?

[*She knows it's too bitter by half as soon as the words clear her lips.* CLINTON *cringes, looking stricken.* JANINE *silently scolds herself.*]

I didn't mean that.

CLINTON: OK.

JANINE: Clint, please.

CLINTON: It's OK.

JANINE: I shouldn't have said it.

CLINTON: I've gotta go. Gas station coming up.

JANINE: OK.

CLINTON: OK, Janine. Bye.

[JANINE *recedes, the lights going down where she stands.* CLINTON *guides the pickup to a stop. He ushers Sammy from the truck, then sets about fueling.*]

CLINTON: Stay close, boy.

[*As* CLINTON *gasses up the truck, a boy, about twelve years old, approaches. He wears a 1970s-style athletic T-shirt, shorts, tube socks that terminate above the knee. This is* BRIAN SHAMLEY.]

CLINTON: Come on, Sammy. [*He lifts the dog back into the cab.*] That's a good boy.

BRIAN: That dog bite?

[CLINTON *turns and faces the boy. Recognition registers on his face.*]

CLINTON: I've never seen him do something like that. Would be a surprise if he did.

BRIAN: Yeah, he looks nice.

CLINTON: Yep.

BRIAN: Can I get a ride?

CLINTON: Sure. It's unlocked. Hop up in there with Sammy.

[CLINTON *and* BRIAN *clamber into the cab of the truck and close their doors.* CLINTON *begins driving.*]

CLINTON: Just cozy up next to Sammy there. He likes people.

[CLINTON *and* BRIAN *share a glance.*]

No offense intended.

BRIAN: Can I ask you something?

CLINTON: Sure. Shoot. Again, no offense.

BRIAN: Where you been?

[CLINTON *deflects as he tries to get a handle on the question.*]

CLINTON: Where we headed?

BRIAN: The neighborhood. Where you been, huh?

CLINTON: Not there. Not in a long time.

BRIAN: But where?

CLINTON: It's a long story. Let's not get into it.

BRIAN: I've been looking for you, that's all. You were nice to me. I liked you.

CLINTON: I wasn't that nice.

BRIAN: Nice enough, especially for an older kid. Nicer than the others. Your mom would give me candy. I liked her, too.

[*Wonder crosses* CLINTON's *face, as if he's seeing something otherworldly. He stops the truck and points.*]

CLINTON: That's the old house.

BRIAN: Yes. And mine next door. I don't know anybody in them now, though.

CLINTON: It wasn't red before. When'd they add the garage?

BRIAN: I don't know.

CLINTON: Sure has changed around here.

BRIAN: Some things. Others, not even a little. Richard Miles still lives up there. [*He points.*]

CLINTON: Richard Miles. Jesus. I haven't thought of him—

BRIAN: I watch him come and go. I'm glad you came. I've been hoping you would.

CLINTON: This isn't a happy place. I didn't want to come back here.

BRIAN: Can I tell you something?

CLINTON: Sure. It's your cab fare.

[BRIAN *looks flummoxed.*]

It's a joke. Tell me.

BRIAN: Don't blame your dad. It wasn't his fault.

CLINTON: I—

BRIAN: He did what anybody would do.

CLINTON: No. I mean, no, he—

BRIAN: I was thankful. Still am, although it doesn't

really matter much now. Thankfulness. It's—[*he searches for a word his boyhood vocabulary can't produce*]

CLINTON: I get it. I understand. It's not just that, you know. It's a whole lifetime. Stuff before and beyond.

BRIAN: Just don't blame him, OK?

CLINTON: It's not that easy, but I'll try.

[CLINTON *gets out of the truck. Prompted by the movement,* BRIAN *does the same. They find their way to the grille and lean against it.*]

CLINTON: I—we—moved to New Mexico not long after. Graduated high school. Went into the Navy. Got out, took a pipelining job up in Billings. Wife. Kid. Ex-wife. Grown kid. You asked. There's the short story.

BRIAN: How old are you?

CLINTON: Forty-six.

BRIAN: I'd be forty-three.

CLINTON: I'm sorry. It shouldn't have happened the way it did.

BRIAN: I'd probably have a beard, like you, huh?

CLINTON: It's a distinct possibility. [*He looks at his watch.*] Listen, I gotta go. It all may be timeless for you, but for me—

BRIAN: Yeah.

[CLINTON *seems caught in indecision; should he shake hands with the boy? Hug him? Or just leave?*]

CLINTON: You want to come with me?

BRIAN: That would be neato. But I can't.

CLINTON: Sure you can. Just hop up there. Sammy liked you well enough.

BRIAN: I have to stay here. I'm not allowed to go places I didn't know. I only knew here.

CLINTON: Allowed?

BRIAN: There's rules and stuff. Where I am, I mean.

[CLINTON *wrenches up his face, confused. A few moments' thought, though, brings the brightness of his having figured something out.*]

BRIAN: I'll be here when you get back.

CLINTON: I'll be sure to stop for gas, then.

[CLINTON *climbs into the cab. The lights fade, leaving* BRIAN *alone to stare wistfully ahead for several seconds, then he steps off the stage.* CLINTON *speaks to the audience from the cab.*]

CLINTON: You'd think they would disturb me, these visitations, or whatever you want to call them. But they don't. They're almost comforting, in a way, because I can feel deep down that whatever space I'm occupying and they're occupying isn't the same, yet we can talk to each other across it. Not that it wasn't jarring the first time my mother showed herself to me. I come home from work one day, walk in the house, Janine's out of town, and there Mom is, sitting in my recliner, talking to me plain as day. Right? I mean, you can't see something like that for the first time and not be just a little thrown off, you know? It's like if you go to your refrigerator, open the door, and see Marilyn Monroe sitting there in the potato salad. You're going to have a thought or two beyond the ordinary, you hear me? But the more she showed up, the more comfortable I got. And seeing Brian? Perfectly natural. [*Chuckles*] That is, perfectly supernatural.

Now, have I ever told anybody, besides Janine, who I pretty much had to tell after she found me jabbering to the air? No, I have not. Nor will I. Especially not a doctor or someone who can decide that I'm not of my right mind and take away the last bit of freedom I've got in this life. I've seen that Travolta flick, where he gets all clairvoyant. I've seen what they do, how they lock you away, think you're nuts. You think if they came to that conclusion about me that they'd let me bust loose and play hide the sausage with Kyra Sedgwick? I think not.

And what if I do have a tumor, like Travolta did in the movie? Would it matter? So I die. So what? Bring it on.

It ain't a tumor, this thing. They're real, all of them. I mean, you saw them, right?

[*The scene dims.*]

Scene Eight

The scene opens with a tight spotlight on CLINTON, *with the rest of the stage shrouded in darkness. A voice comes over the radio as he tunes in.*

RADIO VOICE: The word at this hour is superstorm snow, chasing down from the Canadian border all the way through the Raton Pass between Colorado and New Mexico. If you're south of Cheyenne, Wyoming—[*at this,* CLINTON *says "yep"*]—you're probably ahead of the worst of it. Keep moving south, or hunker down and wait it out…

[CLINTON *shuts off the radio. The spotlight widens, revealing the younger version of* JIMMY COBB *sitting beside him in the passenger seat.* CLINTON *takes notice.*]

CLINTON: And you said I wouldn't make it.

JIMMY: Haven't made it yet, hot shot.

CLINTON: I will. Gonna get you planted—[*at this,* JIMMY *winces*]—and get on with the getting on. As always, Dad, your timing is for shit. You up and die amid the storm of the damn century. You couldn't have waited for spring?

JIMMY: Why the hell should I have waited? Wasn't nothing left to live for anyway.

[*He pats his '70s-era western shirt proudly, impressed with himself.*]

I like this better.

CLINTON: So why're you hanging around here? Get you some of that celestial brew and one of those honky-tonk angels and bask in the hereafter.

JIMMY: You've got a hell of a smart mouth, kid. You ought to be more respectful. I'd have had no truck with you those last years if I hadn't gotten old. Now, I'll never be old again. I oughtta whup you for the things you've said and done.

CLINTON: Try it. Just let me remind you that I'm not the size I was the last time you were wearing those clothes. I'll punch back, old-timer.

JIMMY: Have it your way, Sport. I see that little boy set you straight, told you it wasn't my fault what happened back there.

CLINTON: Yeah, yeah, he told me.

JIMMY: So that's something.

CLINTON: It's a bag of nothing. I'll chalk it up to Brian's eternal youth and inexperience that he just doesn't understand that you—

JIMMY: That man was beating his damn kid, Clinton! I wasn't going to put up with that, no way.

CLINTON: So you just whipped his ass, right there in his front yard, in front of God and his neighbors and everybody? That really helped. Call the fucking cops, man. You humiliated him. It's no wonder he—

JIMMY: So it's my fault he did what he did?

CLINTON: It's not your fault. It's just that you could have made it better, and you made it worse. Like you always do. Did. Thank God for the past tense. Dead family. Boom. We gotta move. Boom. I have to leave the house my mother raised me in—

JIMMY: That move was good for us. It was good that we did it.

CLINTON: Good for you. Not me. You can account for everything however you want now, but you don't get to define anything for me. Got that?

JIMMY: I did what I thought was right.

CLINTON: And you were wrong. Which you can't even imagine, which is the whole damn point. The world is full of cocksure fools and reluctant geniuses. Guess which one you are.

JIMMY: That kid, he was trying to help you. Set your grudge down. You'll sleep better.

CLINTON: I sleep just fine when you're not pestering me, and I'll keep carrying it, thanks. It's instructive. Like I said, he was never old enough to know better. I am.

JIMMY: He knows more than you do. There's clarity out here.

CLINTON: Hasn't filtered down to you yet, I see.

JIMMY: I'm serious.

[*As when he was with* BRIAN, *the recognition of some cosmic truth registers on* CLINTON's *face.*]

CLINTON: Like how now you can only go where you've been?

JIMMY: You know about that?

CLINTON: Brian said something. Took me a while

to figure it out, but makes sense, I guess. As much as anything does. One part I don't get…no, never mind.

JIMMY: What?

CLINTON: I've been seeing Mom for a while.

JIMMY: You have? How long?

CLINTON: Years.

JIMMY: You never said anything.

CLINTON: Yeah. Can you imagine how that would have gone over?

JIMMY: So what's the problem?

CLINTON: Billings. I was never there with her. That's where I've seen her, mostly.

JIMMY: Yeah, but she was there a lot. Hell, when we first got married, I was working on a cattle ranch out in the Pryor Mountains. Billings was the big city. We used to go dancing. Carolina sure could cut a rug.

CLINTON: I never knew about this.

JIMMY: Some things don't belong to you, Mr. Important.

CLINTON: Whatever.

JIMMY: You know where she didn't go?

CLINTON: Where?

JIMMY: Albuquerque. Or New Mexico at all. But I did. As you know. Which means I'll be riding your ass the whole way down. And back, if I take a notion to it. Buckle up, Jack.

CLINTON: I don't know if I can stand that much good luck.

JIMMY: I'll be seeing you, Sport.

[*The spotlight tightens again on* CLINTON, *sending* JIMMY *into darkness. Sammy the dog whines, and* CLINTON *reaches over to reassure him. He then flips on the radio again.*]

RADIO VOICE: State police in Wyoming and Colorado are warning drivers to stay off the highways unless it's a life-and-death situation. Stay in, stay safe, and stay warm.

[CLINTON *turns off the radio again.*]

CLINTON: What the hell is going on here, Sammy?

[*The scene dims.*]

ACT THREE

Scene Nine

The scene opens with KAY *under a single spotlight.*

KAY: The earliest memory I have of my grandfather is from when I was four or five years old. We'd driven down to Albuquerque in the middle of summer, the three of us—Mom, Dad, and me—packed into a 1983 Mercury Cougar without air conditioning, the sickly smell of sweaty bologna sandwiches floating up from the sack lunches riding in the backseat with me. I remember Dad being—not nervous, exactly; I don't have any recall of his being in that particular state. It was more that he was preoccupied. He was hard to talk to on that trip, that I remember. Harder than usual, I mean.

Grandpa Jimmy lived in this squat adobe house just below Juan Tabo Boulevard, a place I found out later he'd bought after his second marriage ended. Her name was Susan; I didn't know her. We spent two or three nights there, Mom and me sleeping on these couches that smelled of stale beer and saltines, Dad on the floor, flopping around all night, all of us sweating in that brick oven of a house.

It was a weird collection of humanity, that much I recall. Dad and Grandpa drank beer and talked about not much. Mom cooked. And I—well, that's the thing. There was nothing in that house for a little girl, so Grandpa dumped out Folger's coffee cans full of coins and had me sort them by denomination. When I was done with those, he dumped tin cans full of bolts and nails and nuts and had me sort those, too. When we left, he gave me the money, over Mom and Dad's objections. Back in Billings, Mom took me to the bank and we opened a savings account with it. There was two-hundred-fifty-three dollars and thirty-seven cents there. The account is still active, still adding interest. I've never touched it. That's weird, right?

And, see, I tell you all that so I can tell you this: The part of that trip that stands out most, all these years later, came on the return drive to Billings, as we passed through Pueblo, Colorado. That town looked, to my young eyes, like glorious, otherworldly ruins—a place that had once prospered and now did not and never would again. All those hard-lived buildings. All those pockmarked streets and clapboard houses and silent mills. It all looked so bombed-out and hollow, and I wanted out of there just as soon as I saw it. I don't know how to explain it, really, the impressions that go deep when you're just a kid, but those are mine, where my grandfather is concerned. Bologna sandwiches. Stacks of change. Dirty nails and bolts. And Pueblo.

So get this. [KAY *pulls a creased sheet of paper from her back pocket and unfolds it.*] If you were to get your hands on the State Patrol reports from Pueblo County, Colorado, from a certain winter day and you were to read with a certain fixation on certain details, you'd learn about a man found sitting against the back wheel of his pickup in the gathering snow, how that man wasn't drunk, wasn't breaking the law, wasn't belligerent, wasn't anything at all except a guy entirely out of place, in a storm entirely out of control, and thus a conundrum to the likes of a highway patrolman, who could only let him continue on his way, as odd as he might have been.

What was Dad doing out there? I'll never know.

I'll always wonder.

[*The spotlight dims on* KAY, *and the lights come up on* CLINTON *and the younger* JIMMY, *in the truck, driving south.*]

JIMMY: Lemme ask you something. Do you remember that bike we got you for Christmas? Jesus, when was that? Seventy-two? Seventy-three? I think it was silver, with an orange seat.

CLINTON: Seventy-three. I remember. Mom passed on the next year.

JIMMY: Is that right? It all runs together.

CLINTON: Not for me, it doesn't.

JIMMY: Yeah, well, give yourself time, Sport. You're just a kid yet.

CLINTON: Sure.

JIMMY: You traded that bike for a different one, didn't you? An older one. A big hunk of junk, as I recall. I remember saying to your mom, "Carolina," I said, "if Crisco was brains, that boy wouldn't grease too big a pan."

CLINTON: Right.

JIMMY: I mean, I knew you was being a damn fool, but I said, "Carolina," I said, "if he wants to make this swap, we've gotta let him do it. Some people need the education that comes with idiocy." That's what I said.

CLINTON: I know you did.

JIMMY: Who was the kid that got that bike, anyway?

CLINTON: You know damn well who it was.

JIMMY: Not that—

CLINTON: Yeah, that kid. Brian. You know why I traded him? Because he didn't get anything for Christmas that year, and he loved that bike more than I ever did the first time he put eyes on it. He had this busted-ass, no-chain five-speed, and I told him, well, hell, kid, I'll swap you if you want.

JIMMY: Well, I—

CLINTON: No, of course not. You never.

[JIMMY *begins to protest, but he's interrupted by sounds from Sammy the dog, sick, heaving sounds that suggest the dog is in extreme pain.*]

JIMMY: Something's wrong with Sammy.

CLINTON: Just a sec—

JIMMY: Pull over, dammit. Something's wrong.

[CLINTON *wheels the truck to the side of the road, opens his door, and hops out.* JIMMY *remains in the cab, in increasing distress.*]

JIMMY: Get him out. Help him, goddammit.

[CLINTON *scrambles around to the other door and pulls the dog to the ground.* JIMMY *slips out, too, and berates his son.*]

JIMMY: What the hell did you feed him?

[*The dog continues to emit horrible sounds as* CLINTON *tends to him.*]

CLINTON: The usual stuff.

JIMMY: What?

CLINTON: Goddamn it, kibble! You know, dog food.

JIMMY: He's dying. Jesus, he's dying.

CLINTON: He's an old dog.

JIMMY: You've killed my damn dog.

CLINTON: He's an old dog.

JIMMY: Asshole dog killer.

[CLINTON *appears beaten down, by the event and by his father's invective. A spotlight comes up on an adjacent stage as* CAROLINA *appears and crosses over to where* CLINTON *and* JIMMY *are.*]

CAROLINA: Clinton, look at me.

[CLINTON *looks up, his eyes meeting his mother's. JIMMY is aware of her presence and watches her as if in awe.*]

CAROLINA: Don't listen to him. It's not your fault. Now be calm and help the dog if you can.

JIMMY: He killed my dog.

CAROLINA: Clinton, you did no such thing.

JIMMY: You always took his side, didn't you?

CAROLINA: Just shut up, Jimmy.

[CLINTON *continues tending to the dog, who at last makes a vomiting sound, ejecting something, and then pants heavily.*]

CLINTON: He's OK. [*He peers down, his face registering revulsion.*] Looks like he found a dead bird and ate it.

CAROLINA: Goodness.

[CLINTON *coaxes Sammy into the truck as* JIMMY *comes toward them as if to take over.*]

CLINTON: No. Just stay away. I've got him.

JIMMY: He's my dog.

CLINTON: You don't have anything to say about it anymore.

[CLINTON *eases Sammy into the cab and closes the door. He returns to* JIMMY *and* CAROLINA, *who are standing there and looking at each other silently and warily.*]

JIMMY: I was just—

CLINTON: I don't want to hear another word. How in the world you're more trouble to me dead than you ever were alive is beyond me. I must have really pissed off somebody powerful.

CAROLINA: Don't talk like that. You don't even know.

CLINTON: No, I certainly don't.

[*He turns now, fiercely, toward his father.*]

I want you out of here. Leave me be. Leave me to Mom.

JIMMY: I'll go. But she's got to go first.

CLINTON: No.

CAROLINA: Yes.

[CLINTON *looks at her, betrayed.*]

CLINTON: Why?

CAROLINA: It's his moment, Clinton. There are rules, like I told you before. I broke them by intruding. He was here first. It's his call.

CLINTON: It's *my* call.

JIMMY: It doesn't work that way, Sport.

CLINTON: Oh, so now you're the expert on how it works? [JIMMY *shrugs.*]

CAROLINA: He's right. He could have me sanctioned for being here at all. [*At this,* JIMMY *claps his hands together. She looks at him in a withering way, and he casts eyes downward.*] But he's not going to say one word about this, and we're both going to leave and give you some peace. I have to go.

[JIMMY *doesn't say anything, and she seems satisfied by the non-response.*]

CLINTON: I don't want you to go.

CAROLINA: I'm sorry. We'll see each other again. Just not right now. [*The light goes off her and she leaves.*]

JIMMY: Just you and me.

CLINTON: Go.

JIMMY: Look, Sport…

CLINTON: Go!

[*The light on* JIMMY *dims.*]

JIMMY: I'll be seeing you, kid.

[*His mother and father gone,* CLINTON *looks around, despairing, and at last slumps to the ground against the back wheel of the pickup. He draws up his knees, puts his arms across them, sets his head down and cries as red-and-blue strobes flood the scene. After a few seconds of this, the stage goes dark and* KAY *steps into a spotlight on the adjacent stage. She begins reading from the earlier piece of paper.*]

KAY: Here's what an Officer Jonathon Hunter of the Colorado Highway Patrol wrote in the report he submitted to his watch commander.

[OFFICER HUNTER *steps out, speaks, then recedes.*]

OFFICER HUNTER: The subject, Clinton Cobb, 46, of Billings, Montana, said that his father's dog got sick and he pulled over to attend to the animal. Without prompting, he said he was transporting his deceased father in the back of the pickup and was trying to get him to Albuquerque for burial. He produced paperwork to this effect, and I called the mortuary in Billings and verified that Mr. Cobb had authorization to take the body. I did not verify the remains in the pickup. Asked why he was sitting in the snow, Mr. Cobb said he was overcome by grief and was taking a few minutes to gather himself. I advised him that he should not be traveling in these conditions and that he would be taking matters into his own hands if he remained on the road. He said he understood but needed to continue. I had no reason to detain him. I advised Mr. Cobb that the weather should improve below Raton Pass and wished him well.

KAY: That is what I know. It is at once informative and utterly absent of anything useful. I know my father made it to Albuquerque, which is the important part, I guess. There's nothing in the record that I can find between Pueblo and Albuquerque that offers any clue to what came next. Or didn't. Dad and I had one more conversation. We'll get to that soon enough.

I wish there'd been more. That's the biggest loss. We should've had time, and we didn't, and nobody can repay that. Am I bitter? No, I don't think so. I'm sad. I'm hurt. I'm lacking in the information that can connect what I knew then to what I can only imagine now.

I miss my dad something fierce.

[*The scene dims.*]

Scene Ten

The scene opens with a small crowd, eight or ten people, mostly men, mingling, beers and mixed drinks in hand. CLINTON *and the younger* JIMMY *stand midstage, with* CLINTON *engaged in conversation with an older gentleman,* GIL ALLEN.

CLINTON: This is something else, Gil. I never expected it. Can't thank you enough for hosting.

GIL: Glad to do it. Glad you called and let me know.

[JIMMY *eyes* GIL *suspiciously and leans in to* CLINTON.]

JIMMY: Ask him how the fuck he's still standing upright. He was half-dead thirty years ago.

[CLINTON *winces but otherwise ignores* JIMMY.]

CLINTON: Everybody here knew Dad, huh?

GIL: Most of them, yeah. Some of the younger fellers, the guys your age, their daddies were friends of Jimmy's. He wasn't the first of our bunch to go, sad to say.

JIMMY: Should have been the last. [*He moves off, to examine some of the people in the room.*]

CLINTON: Well, it's a hell of a nice thing. I was afraid there wouldn't be anybody tomorrow. I had no idea he had this many friends left down here.

GIL: Yeah, we're fond of ol' Jimmy. Sorry to be saying goodbye. But, you know, it happens. Faster'n you think it will.

CLINTON: Sure.

[*JIMMY dashes back to tell CLINTON something.*]

JIMMY: Phyllis Goddamn Flanagan. Hot damn! I never could time up being single when she was, but there she is, widowed and free, and here I am, looking as good as I ever have, and we can't make the hookup. Man, what a raw deal this dying shit is.

CLINTON: Shut up!

GIL: Pardon?

CLINTON: Nothing.

[CLINTON *and* GIL *stare at their beers. It's been a number of years since they've seen each other, and the conversational well is draining quickly.*]

GIL: Meant to ask you: What's your plan for that dog?

[GIL *motions to Sammy, snoozing in a corner of the room.*]

CLINTON: Sammy?

GIL: Yeah.

CLINTON: God, I haven't thought it through, to be honest. Take him back and figure it out, I guess. I always hoped the dog would go first, to tell you the truth. Dog first, Dad to follow, a clean ending. Does that sound crass? I don't mean to sound crass.

JIMMY: What the hell kind of hope is that?

GIL: Not especially, no. I hear you. You inclined to part with him?

CLINTON: You inclined to take him on?

[JIMMY *fixates on* GIL.]

JIMMY: Yeah, are you inclined to take him on?

GIL: I think I'd like to, yeah. Been some years since

I've had an animal. Belle didn't like dogs too much. She's gone now. It's lonely. If Jimmy liked him, I'd like the old boy, too, I reckon. Yeah, I'd take him. If you don't want him.

CLINTON: I'd be proud to let you have Sammy.

JIMMY: Yeah, we'd be proud. [*He turns dismissive.*] Sammy doesn't even like this so-called son of mine.

GIL: Well, that'd just be fine. [*He extends a hand, which* CLINTON *shakes heartily.*]

CLINTON: I'll go get his stuff out of the truck, just so I don't forget.

[CLINTON *and* JIMMY *move to the stage with the pickup.* CLINTON *stops short of the vehicle and turns to his father.*]

CLINTON: Listen, Dad, do you suppose you could give me a second here? I'd like to make a call.

JIMMY: Gonna get you a nice piece of ass?

CLINTON: Yeah, that's it. You know me so well.

[JIMMY *grabs himself lewdly.*]

JIMMY: Equipment still work?

CLINTON: Not that it's any of your business, Dad—

JIMMY: Here we go.

CLINTON: —but I was thinking maybe I'd call my daughter. You remember Katey, right? You've seen pictures.

[*This amuses* JIMMY.]

JIMMY: I'll give you credit, Sport. You are consistent. Consistently a prick.

CLINTON: High praise from the likes of you.

JIMMY: OK, Sport, have it your way. [*He nods toward the party.*] Better brand of people back there anyway.

[JIMMY *turns and heads back to the soiree.*]

CLINTON: Don't keep 'em waiting, superstar.

[JIMMY *gives a wave without turning around.* CLINTON *watches until he's out of sight, then pulls his cellphone from a pocket and begins dialing. On an adjacent stage,* KAY *steps into a spotlight.*]

KAY: Dad. Hi.

CLINTON: Hi, there, pookie nose.

KAY: Dad, are you calling from 1996? What's with the pookie-nose crap?

CLINTON: I am calling from Albuquerque.

KAY: I see.

CLINTON: Funeral's tomorrow.

KAY: I've heard.

CLINTON: Come down in the morning. Get a flight. I'm sorry I didn't ask you to come before.

KAY: Dad. There's work—

CLINTON: Please. I don't want to beg. But come. I need you here. We're going to send him off. You should be here.

[KAY *gets suddenly emotional.*]

KAY: I want to. I don't know. Why couldn't you have asked me before?

CLINTON: I just didn't see it, OK? Thought I was doing you a favor, keeping you away from it. But I was wrong. You're going to have to do this for me someday. Consider it a training exercise.

KAY: Dad, stop.

CLINTON: Funeral's at three. There's plenty of time. Hop a morning flight. We'll drive back together. Like old times. We'll eat crap food and listen to music. It'll be fun.

KAY: I'll try. I promise, I'll try. OK?

CLINTON: Thanks, Katey.

[KAY *begins to correct him, but* CLINTON *interrupts.*]

Kay. Sorry, sweetheart. I'm trying.

KAY: I know you are. I love you, Dad.

CLINTON: Love you.

[*They hang up, and the spotlight leaves* KAY. CLINTON *considers things a moment, then dials another number.* JANINE *steps into the spot* KAY *has vacated, under a spotlight, answers her ringing phone.*]

JANINE: Hi, Clint. Everything OK?

CLINTON: It is, yeah. Strangely enough. Gil Allen threw a little get-together of Dad's friends. It's a nice little sendoff.

JANINE: Aw, he would have liked that.

CLINTON: Adjust your tense. He is liking it.

JANINE: He's there?

CLINTON: Unless my eyes deceive me. Which, now that I think of it…

JANINE: Entirely possible!

[*They laugh together, a good kind of laugh that speaks to the history they share.*]

CLINTON: No, it's been good. Made me feel less like this was a fool's errand. It's like a benediction, only with cheap beer.

JANINE: I'm glad. I really am.

CLINTON: I called Katey.

JANINE: OK.

CLINTON: Asked her to fly down in the morning. It stopped snowing?

JANINE: A few hours ago. Is she gonna do it?

CLINTON: I don't know. I hope so. She was resistant. Crying, I think.

JANINE: Well, you can't blame her.

CLINTON: I don't.

JANINE: I'll call her.

CLINTON: Don't tell her I asked you to. I want her to come only if she wants to. No pressure.

JANINE: You should know by now that she can't be made to do anything. If you see her, it'll be because she made her own call.

CLINTON: I know.

JANINE: It's the best thing about her. And I don't know where it came from. She didn't get it from either of us, I don't think.

CLINTON: I know.

JANINE: She'll come, Clint. I think she will. Rest easy tonight.

CLINTON: You sure?

JANINE: Been a long time since I've been sure about anything. I've got a feeling, that's all.

CLINTON: OK.

JANINE: You having fun tonight?

CLINTON: It's a kick, yeah. The old goat still has a lot of friends down this way. Surprised they never came to see him, or he never came back down here when he still could. You listen to 'em and think, hell, I don't know this cat they're talking about. Sounds like a hell of a guy. Isn't that funny?

JANINE: He always did have another side of life that he kept pretty well out of sight.

CLINTON: Anyway, I'm going back in. Thanks for talking me down a little bit. I'll look for Katey. Tell her to call me if she decides to come and needs picking up.

JANINE: I will. Clint? [*She begins choking up.*]

CLINTON: Yeah?

JANINE: I…I want you to know…I— [*She can't finish the thought.* CLINTON *struggles for his own control.*]

CLINTON: I know. Me, too. Night now.

[*They hang up.* CLINTON *gathers up a leash, a bag of dog food, and a dog bed, and he heads back to the soiree. Once in, he sets them down, then has another handshake with* GIL. JIMMY *is at the center of the room, observing.* CLINTON *finds a can of beer and chugs it. He makes his way around the room, backslapping and talking, a friend to everyone, it seems, as if his spirit and sense of fun have been loosened by the atmosphere and the infusion of alcohol. As* CLINTON *makes friends,* JIMMY *edges to one side of the room, farther away from the crowd. Someone hands* CLINTON *another beer, and he chugs that, too.* JIMMY's *mood darkens at the same rate that* CLINTON's *becomes luminous, until* JIMMY *is all alone to the side and* CLINTON *is the center of attention.* CLINTON *finds him with his eyes and points, derisively.* JIMMY *fumes. The party goes on. And the scene dims.*]

ACT FOUR

Scene Eleven

The scene opens with CLINTON *in bed, slowly emerging from slumber.* JIMMY, *the younger version, sits reverse-saddle in a chair at the foot of the bed, eyeballing his son, a hardness to his gaze and a rigidity to his pose.* GIL *comes in carrying a blanket.* CLINTON *emerges, blinking, from sleep.*

GIL: I didn't mean to wake you.

[CLINTON *stretches, feeling the tingle.*]

CLINTON: You didn't.

GIL: Brought an extra blanket. Cold morning. A good, hard freeze. [*He sets the blanket on the bed.* CLINTON *comes the rest of the way out of sleep. He* *looks at* JIMMY, *whose gaze hasn't shifted, and back to* GIL.]

CLINTON: What the hell happened?

GIL: Jose Cuervo ain't much of a friend, is he?

[CLINTON, *ashamed, covers his face with his hand.*]

CLINTON: Not when you're riding the Budweiser Clydesdale, no.

JIMMY: Lightweight.

[CLINTON *swings his legs off the bed and prepares to get up.*]

CLINTON: What time is it?

GIL: A little after eight. Hungry?

CLINTON: Not so much, no. [*He looks at his father, who's staring back.* CLINTON *shifts his body, uncomfortable.*]

GIL: Meant to tell you last night. I reached out to Susan. Thought she might want to at least know about your dad.

CLINTON: Susan?

[JIMMY, *also aroused at the mention, stands from the chair and paces toward* GIL.]

GIL: Yeah. Talked to her son.

CLINTON: Keith.

GIL: Yeah, that's him. She's in a bad way, he said. Told me he'd let her know, not that she'd understand it.

CLINTON: She's here in town?

JIMMY: Leave it be.

GIL: Little house over on Candelaria. Been there for years.

CLINTON: You got the address?

JIMMY: Leave it be!

GIL: 1617. Easy to remember. You know, after she and Jimmy busted up, she'd still call me when she had a plugged drain or something. Haven't seen her in years, though, not since I retired. Nice lady. A shame about her. Dementia, sounds like. Been a lot of that these last few years. Lost a lot of folks. She was a good lady.

[JIMMY *moves toward* GIL, *getting in his face.*]

JIMMY: What the hell would you know about it?

[CLINTON *pulls on his socks and boots and gets into his jacket. He has slept in his clothes.*]

CLINTON: 1617, you say?

[JIMMY *paces back to* CLINTON, *who is moving away from him.* JIMMY *is seething now.*]

JIMMY: You don't fucking dare.

CLINTON: I'll be back before it's time to go to the service.

GIL: Did I do something wrong?

[JIMMY *turns on him.*]

JIMMY: Yes!

CLINTON: No. I guess…you know, maybe I ought to just say goodbye while I have the chance. I haven't thought of her in years.

JIMMY: Maybe you ought to just sit your ass down.

[CLINTON *regards him with a blank face, as if he's looking through his father.*]

GIL: OK.

CLINTON: I'll be back.

STRAIGHT ON TO STARDUST

JIMMY: I forbid this.

CLINTON: I'll be back.

[*The scene goes dark as* CLINTON, JIMMY *and* GIL *leave the stage. On an adjacent stage,* KAY *steps forward into a single spotlight and takes a seat in what appears to be an airline chair.*]

KAY: Spoiler alert: He doesn't come back.

I'm oblivious to all of this, of course. I'm in the air now, Billings to Denver, Denver to Albuquerque. I have a stomach that won't stop flipping and flopping. The nice flight attendant gives me ginger ale. [*A woman enters and hands* KAY *a clear plastic cup filled with a beverage, which* KAY *accepts gratefully.*] On the second flight, I have a row to myself. It's not all bad.

We arrive in Albuquerque. [KAY *stands and the airline seat is whisked away, replaced by a car's bench seat. She sits down.*] I take a cab to the funeral home. I call Dad and it goes to voicemail. "Dad, I'm here and on my way. I will meet you at the service. I love you."

[KAY *stands again and the bench seat is whisked away. A casket is rolled in along with a single chair.*]

It's early. I'm early. I'm also entirely too late. I sit with my grandpa. He has nothing to say. I have even less.

[KAY *sits down in a single chair next to the casket. She puts her hand on the wood finish. She leans her head against it and she closes her eyes.*]

I barely even knew you. I'm sorry.

You barely even knew me. Are you sorry?

[KAY *stands yet again. The casket is wheeled to the side. Guests, the same people from the party the night before, flood the stage.* KAY *begins shaking hands and accepting hugs.*]

Everybody says nice things about Grandpa, about how much they liked him, and I can't help but wonder if they're talking about the same man I didn't know. Everybody asks where Dad is. What can I tell them? I do not know. Then, now, tomorrow. I do not know.

[GIL *steps to* KAY. *He hugs her as he might his own granddaughter.*]

GIL: I'm sure he got hung up somehow. He wouldn't have missed this for anything.

KAY: But he did.

GIL: I'm sure he didn't intend to.

[GIL *hugs her again and leaves the stage, along with the other guests.* KAY *addresses the audience.*]

KAY: But he did.

There are nearly 600,000 people in Albuquerque, New Mexico. We can't find a one who saw Dad after he stopped to see Grandpa's old wife. We know he was there. We know he left. But where did he go, and why?

Stop me if you've heard this one before: We. Do. Not. Know.

[*The car seat returns to the stage.* KAY *sits down.*]

I rode a cab back to the airport. [KAY *stands and the car seat is removed.*] I bought a ticket home. [*The airline seat returns to the stage.* KAY *sits down again.*] I flew back to Billings. What else could I do? He beckoned me. I came. And he went somewhere else, for reasons that are entirely his own and entirely shrouded in mystery for anyone who loves him.

[KAY *is emotional now.*]

This is not my fault. I will not let this be my fault.

[KAY *stands and the airline seat is removed from the stage.*]

Daddy, where did you go?

[*The scene dims.*]

Scene Twelve

The scene opens in a dimly lit bedroom. The erstwhile SUSAN COBB lies in bed, eyes closed, serene and unresponsive. CLINTON sits at her bedside, facing the audience, close enough to speak softly, but also at a pronounced distance. He is not looking at her with human warmth. JIMMY, still the younger version, paces the room, agitating. With each line CLINTON speaks, JIMMY stops and answers, as if it is a call-and-response series, then resumes his pacing.

CLINTON: You're so old.

JIMMY: You're so old, too, Sport, if you haven't noticed. I'm the only young one here. Let's go now and leave her to her dignity.

CLINTON: I never thought I'd see you again.

JIMMY: She's a shell, a vessel, most of the way to a corpse. You ain't seeing her. Let's go, damn you.

CLINTON: I never wanted to see you again.

JIMMY: So let's go.

CLINTON: I've tried to forgive you.

JIMMY: You had nothing to forgive. Don't you fucking turn this on her at the end when she's got nothing to say and no way to say it. Don't you do that.

CLINTON: Things were taken from me, things I couldn't get back, things I didn't have to give when it was my time to offer them to someone else. You took that from me.

JIMMY: You took! You took everything!

CLINTON: I was fifteen. I trusted you. I wanted to trust you.

JIMMY: You knew what you were doing.

CLINTON: I wanted love.

JIMMY: See? See?

CLINTON: I didn't want what you offered me.

JIMMY: Lie!

CLINTON: I didn't know what to do with that. I

didn't know how to let it go once I had it. The shame of it. God, the shame of it.

JIMMY: You didn't want to let it go. I had to do what needed doing. I had to do it!

CLINTON: It's why he hates me.

JIMMY: You're goddamned right.

CLINTON: I couldn't tell them I was sorry. I couldn't tell them why. I couldn't tell them how I'd become half of what I needed to be.

JIMMY: You ain't sorry.

CLINTON: I'm sorry.

JIMMY: You're not. You lie now, the way you lied then.

[CLINTON *at last succumbs to his buried grief, putting his head in his hands and weeping.* JIMMY *stands to his side, at a distance, ashamed of the weakness he sees.*]

JIMMY: You're pathetic. You've always been pathetic. I tried to cut you loose from your mother's apron strings for fear they'd choke you to death, same as I had to cut her loose from what bound her. But you, you were already long gone, useless as a boy, a son, and now a bag of nothing as a man. I couldn't give you what you needed then. And what you took from me later…[*He motions to the prone woman in bed.*]… What you took from her, I'll never forgive. You live your life in selfishness. I am ashamed of you. I am ashamed that you carry my name. I am ashamed that my good blood courses through you.

[CLINTON *takes all of this, head down. When* JIMMY *finishes, he stays covered up a beat or two, then lifts his head.*]

CLINTON: Is that why you're here? To punish me? You didn't get enough of those shots in while you were still kicking? You have to follow me now and dole out some more?

JIMMY: It'll never be enough. Not for what you did.

[CLINTON *looks back to* SUSAN.]

CLINTON: I was just a boy. She knew what she was doing. I didn't.

JIMMY: You sure enough did it anyway, didn't you?

CLINTON: I was just a boy.

[CLINTON *and* JIMMY *are through with the exchange. They look at each other for a few seconds, then* CLINTON's *features reflect astonishment, as if he's figured something out.*]

CLINTON: Why didn't you take Mom back to Texas when she died, like she asked you to?

JIMMY: Fuck Texas.

CLINTON: Why didn't we ever go as a family to see Grandma and Grandpa? Why'd they always have to come to us?

JIMMY: Fuck Texas. It ain't about Texas. Your mother lived in Wyoming. She was gone. Wyoming dirt was good enough to hold her.

[CLINTON *consider this a second or two, then brightens with awareness.*]

CLINTON: You've never been there.

[JIMMY *steps toward his son but can't corral his words.* CLINTON *turns away and faces the audience, to whom he now speaks.*]

Amarillo's, what, five hours from here? That's where Mom was from. Amarillo! When I was a little boy, a couple of times we drove down, just her and me, and we went there together. She's been there. The cosmic traces of her, they're in that Texas air, and I could find her there. I bet I could.

[JIMMY *comes up behind* CLINTON, *reaching for him.*]

JIMMY: Listen—

[CLINTON *moves farther away.*]

CLINTON: Amarillo! It's five hours from here. Five hours! And that's it, isn't it? I cut myself loose from this, and I go to her, and that's how it will be forevermore.

JIMMY: Son—

CLINTON: Five hours! By God, that's it. Amarillo by midafternoon, as the song goes…

JIMMY: Clinton!

[CLINTON, *practically giddy, heads to the exit of the stage, then looks back at* JIMMY.]

CLINTON: So long, Dad. Have a nice afterlife.

[CLINTON *completes his exit.* JIMMY, *struck dumb, stands there, watching, for a few seconds. At last, he turns away and goes to occupy the bedside seat that had held his son. He looks at* SUSAN *for a bit, almost repelled by her age and infirmity. Finally, he clasps her hands together across her chest and pats them.*]

JIMMY: I'll see you soon, sweetheart.

[*The scene dims.*]

Epilogue—Scene Thirteen

The scene opens as KAY *comes to center stage and stands under a single spotlight.*

KAY: For a few months after the funeral, I'd call his number to see if he would pick up. For a while, it rang through before heading to voicemail. Later, after the charge was gone, I guess, straight to voicemail.

[KAY *dials a number and listens to a message.*]

Hey, this here's Clinton Cobb. I either can't talk to you or don't want to talk to you, pick the one that applies, then leave me a message and we'll see if I call you back. And then you'll know for sure.

KAY: He had that message for years. I always told him it was unprofessional and a little insulting, but you know my dad—you can't tell him anything. Not now, anyway, if you ever could. Anyway, eventually, I got on with it. What choice did I have? He left us and went…somewhere. Meanwhile, I have to stay and get on with the life that belongs to me.

The great mystery, of course, is this: Is he out there somewhere?

I think he is. Mom thinks he is.

[*A spotlight on the adjacent stage lands on* JANINE, *who stands holding a stack of mail. She sorts through it, until she finds a postcard, which draws a wide smile from her. She clutches it to her chest and the spotlight fades.*]

KAY: The postcards arrive irregularly, a pattern of mailing and outbound geography that can't be reconciled. The postmarks are Marfa, Texas, and Hot Springs, Arkansas, and Owensboro, Kentucky, and other places, too. No words. Hearts, sometimes. Little drawings that I take to be me, or Mom. Clues, I guess, if you're into games. I've given up games. You can't win at them.

[*While* KAY *continues talking, a light comes up on the stage with the pickup truck. In it,* CLINTON *and* CAROLINA *ride together, laughing, a joy between them, as* KAY *finishes.*]

Something chased him out of our lives and into the gaping maw of the world. Something got at him and wouldn't let him go, until he let go of his own volition. I wish I knew what it was. I wish he'd talked to me before he left. But I could wish for a lot of things and harvest nothing but disappointment. Better to take things as they come. Or don't. It's not up to me, anyway.

He knows where we are. He knows how to find us. Earlier this year, we celebrated his birthday. We celebrated him. I made a birthday wish for him by proxy. I bet you know what it was.

[JANINE *joins* KAY. *She holds a birthday cake. Together, they blow out a candle atop it.* JANINE *exits.*]

Maybe someday, some way, he will find his way back to us. Maybe he'll want to, and he'll do it. At the same time, I've given up hope that we'll hear from him—a hope like that, it cuts you too deeply while you're waiting for fruition. Let's just say I'm open to it. Let's just say I'm here. Let's just say I'm prepared to let the past go for the promise of the future.

[KAY *stops and considers her next words.*]

Let's just say a little spark goes off in the chambers of my heart every time…

[KAY's *cellphone rings. She looks at it. She smiles widely. She holds it to her ear.*]

KAY: Hello?

[*The scene goes dark. The end.*]

Author's Note

This play you hold in your hands stands as an example of how a creative effort often resolves itself outside the will or wants of the creator.

I wanted *Straight On To Stardust* to be a novel. Got well down the road with that desire, then the writing had a different idea. It opted to up and die, right there, mid-story.

This sort of thing happens more often than I'm comfortable with, and more often than I ever thought it would before I started doing such things. So I followed the only protocol left to me: I stashed it in the guts of my hard drive and let it sit in incompleteness.

It might still be there if not for my indulgence in one of the true pleasures of life: I went to the theater. Specifically, I went to see Yellowstone Repertory Theatre's production of *The Glass Menagerie* in the spring of 2018.

I absorbed that show not just as an audience member, which would have been plenty powerful on its own, but also as a guy who writes stories and enjoys picking apart the ways others go about that business.

Something about this great Tennessee Williams play captivated me. The exposition, the breaking of the wall between cast and audience, things that would be audacious, even ill-advised in prose—those were the very things that made the play. I went home that night thinking I'd sure like to write something similar. Let me be clear that I'm talking about form here, not the aspiration toward literary achievement. I'll borrow a phrase heavyweight boxer Larry Holmes made famous: I couldn't carry Tennessee Williams' jockstrap. (Holmes said it in defiance, after the first loss of his professional career. I say it in reverence and with a healthy dollop of self-awareness.)

It was some months after that production, when we were living in Maine and my creative reserves for writing novels had gone temporarily dry, that I realized I had a likely play candidate in my abandoned files. Out came *Straight On To Stardust*, this time with a new purpose.

I'm grateful to Craig Huisenga and the cast and board of directors at Yellowstone Rep for going the full route with this play: doing a Zoom read at the height of the pandemic, graduating to a table read at This House of Books in Billings in April 2022, and finally for giving it a world premiere as the opener for a new season. At every step, they've made it better through their professionalism and their well-considered notes that have sent me back to the writing table, again and again. It's been a great privilege to watch them take words on a page and turn them into something that can be watched and deeply felt.

I'm grateful to This House of Books for the way it champions art in Billings. Please support independent bookstores, wherever they are and wherever you are. They are vital cultural hubs.

I'm grateful for the home team—Elisa and Spatz the cat and Fretless, the world's most ironically named dog. It's hard to make the rest of it go without your support.

I'm grateful to you for buying and reading this play. Want to put it on? My gratitude abounds, and I look forward to hearing from you.

Craig Lancaster
Billings, Montana

www.ingramcontent.com/pod-product-compliance
Lightning Source LLC
LaVergne TN
LVHW092053060526
838201LV00047B/1373